**Walrus in association with
Theatre Royal Plymouth**

presents

T0286389

A

TABLE

TENNIS

PLAY

Sam Steiner

A Table Tennis Play was first performed on 1 August 2019 at the
Underbelly, Edinburgh, as part of the Edinburgh Festival Fringe.

A
TABLE
TENNIS
PLAY

Sam Steiner

Cast

MIA	Beth Holmes
CALLUM	Euan Kitson
CATH	Rosa Robson

Creative Team

Director	Ed Madden
Designer	Lizzy Leech
Lighting Designer	Charlotte Burton
Sound Designer	Richard Bell
Casting Consultant	Christopher Worrall

Foreword – Ed Madden, director

The first production on which Sam and I collaborated took five months to get from genesis to premiere. It changed and grew a huge amount over the course of several iterations following its first performances, but its initial journey from something which barely existed in our heads to something very much happening in front of an audience was almost inconceivably brief.

Not so this time around. We first spoke about the bare bones of the idea which would eventually become the play you are holding now in September 2015. We were in a warehouse in Manchester, we were playing table tennis, and no doubt Sam was winning. In the years since, various other ideas have come and gone but this one stuck, and gradually evolved. The process has been slow and fitful and has occasionally felt a touch impossible, but to my mind the resulting play justifies the climb. As irritatingly good as Sam continues to be at receiving perfectly good serves and converting them into devastating returns, so he is somehow able to take the nub of a concept and shape it in rich and unexpected ways.

As we rehearse, that shaping continues apace. The play is in no small part about the possibility of change in certain real and imaginative spaces, and since rehearsal rooms are both of those things, it feels right that some of the text's most potent moments have sprung from our time spent with three brilliant actors on the sixth floor of an office building in London Bridge. I write this at the end of week two of rehearsals, as challenged and excited as I have ever been by a project, already anxious for Monday to roll around so we can dive back in.

A Table Tennis Play represents a conscious attempt to write a one-act play which eschews breakneck pacing in favour of restraint and quietude. It is a coming-of-age play which wonders when we actually come of age; a play about connection and empathy which for my money is also an examination of loss, and perhaps a kind of ghost story to boot. Its still waters run fathoms deep, and I am enormously proud to be directing it.

July 2019

Biographies

Walrus

Walrus is a theatre company dedicated to new writing. The company's award-winning debut show *Lemons Lemons Lemons Lemons Lemons* premiered at Warwick Arts Centre in 2015. The production subsequently sold out three consecutive Edinburgh Fringe runs and completed a major UK tour to venues including Theatre Royal Plymouth, HOME Manchester, Camden People's Theatre and Sheffield Crucible. The company's style is formally innovative, theatrically intimate, and concerned with finding new ways to stage our relationship with the world around us.

Richard Bell (Sound Designer)

Theatre as sound designer: *The Ladykillers, Beauty and the Beast* (Theatre by the Lake); *Single Spies* (Theatre by the Lake/York Theatre Royal), *The Game of Love and Chai* (Tara Arts); *The End of Hope* (Soho); *Dolphins and Sharks, Windows* (Finborough); *Hyem* (Theatre503); *MA Directors' Festival 2017* (Orange Tree); *Birthday Suit* (Old Red Lion); *Wet Bread* (Sheer Drop).

Theatre as associate sound designer: *The Space Shed* (Unlimited); *Misty* (Bush/Trafalgar Studios); *Hogarth's Progress* (Rose); *Baskerville* (Liverpool Playhouse); *Loot* (Watermill); *My Eyes Went Dark* (59E59, New York); *1984* (Playhouse Theatre/Australian tour/Singapore International Festival of Arts); *The Lottery of Love, Blue Heart* (Orange Tree); *Frankenstein* (Wilton's Music Hall); *Years of Sunlight* (Theatre503); *One for Sorrow, The Children* (Royal Court); *Peter Pan Goes Wrong* (Apollo); *I Call My Brothers, Diary of a Madman, The Iphigenia Quartet* (Gate); *A High Street Odyssey* (Inspector Sands).

Other media as sound designer: Zombies, Run! Season 1 & 2 (Six to Start, Android/iPhone app)

Charlotte Burton (Lighting Designer)

Charlotte trained at LIPA where she was awarded the prize for Creative & Technical Excellence.

Design credits include: *Memoirs of an Asian Football Casual* (Curve); *Bugsy Malone, The Blue Road, Vinegar Tom, Posh, Pornography, Hacktivists* (Royal & Derngate).

Associate credits include: *The Son* (Duke of York's, West End); *Jude* (Hampstead); *My Name is Lucy Barton* (Bridge); *La Clamenza di Tito* (Opera de Oviedo); *Long Day's Journey Into Night* (Wyndham's, West End/BAM, New York/The Wallis, LA); *Jubilee* (Lyric Hammersmith).

Assistant credits include: *Joseph and the Amazing Technicolour Dreamcoat, Cinderella* (London Palladium); *Olivier Awards 2019* (Royal Albert Hall); *Annie* (Piccadilly, West End/UK tour); *Young Frankenstein* (Garrick, West End/ Newcastle Theatre Royal); *Sunset Boulevard, An Officer and a Gentleman, The Wedding Singer, The Addams Family* (UK tour); *The Children* (Royal Court).

Charlotte was the inaugural participant of the Lumiere Scheme run by the Association of Lighting Designers.

Beth Holmes (Mia)

For Walrus: *Lemons Lemons Lemons Lemons Lemons.*

Other theatre includes: *Enveloped in Velvet* (Ransack Theatre at Flow Salford); *Road* (Warwick Arts Centre/NSDF).

Television includes: *Doctors* (BBC).

Beth is a co-founder of Walrus.

Euan Kitson (Callum)

Euan trained at the Royal Welsh College of Music and Drama.

For Walrus: *Lemons Lemons Lemons Lemons Lemons.*

Other theatre includes: *Elton John's Glasses* (Watford Palace); *Some People Talk About Violence* (Barrel Organ with The Hub/Camden People's Theatre/Warwick Arts Centre); *Nothing* (Barrel Organ); *Slick* (NYT).

Film includes: *Earthbound* (Little Blue Dot); *Tyler* (Bryony Davies).

Euan is a founder member of Barrel Organ and co-founder of Walrus.

Lizzy Leech (Designer)

Lizzy trained at Bristol Old Vic Theatre School and studied English Literature at Warwick University.

Recent designs include: *The Merchant of Venice* (Stafford Festival Shakespeare); *Cymbeline* (Royal Central School of Speech and Drama); *The Butterfly Lion* (The Barn Theatre, Cirencester); *Hansel and Gretel, Fairytale Detectives* (Theatr Clwyd); *Songlines* (HighTide); *The Leftovers* (Leicester Curve); *A Girl In School Uniform (Walks Into A Bar)* (New Diorama Theatre/Leeds Playhouse); *Alby the Penguin Saves Christmas* (Oxford Playhouse); *Noye's Fludde* (Blackheath Halls Children's Opera); *Don Giovanni* (Waterperry Opera Festival); *Vanity Fair* (Middle Temple Hall); *Love for Love, The Heresy of Love* (Bristol Old Vic).

As assistant designer: *Pericles* (National Theatre); *Beginning* (National Theatre/West End); *Macbeth* (Royal Shakespeare Company); *A Tale of Two Cities, Oliver Twist* (Regent's Park Open Air Theatre).

Ed Madden (Director)

For Walrus: *Lemons Lemons Lemons Lemons Lemons.*

Other theatre includes, as director: *A Number* (The Other Room); *The World's Wife* (WNO and touring).

As staff/assistant director: *Tartuffe* (National Theatre); *The Winter's Tale* (Shakespeare's Globe); *The Children* (Royal Court); *The Rivals* (Bristol Old Vic/Glasgow Citizens,/Liverpool Everyman & Playhouse); *The Iphigenia Quartet* (Gate).

Ed is a co-founder of Walrus and recipient of a Leverhulme Arts Scholarship.

Rosa Robson (Cath)

Rosa trained at Ecole Philippe Gaulier.

Theatre includes: *Don Quixote* (Garrick); *Siren* (Pleasance Dome); *Dr Faustus, The Alchemist* (RSC).

Television includes: *Nick Helm's Heavy Entertainment* (BBC).

Film includes: *Black Mountain Poets* (Film4).

Rosa is also one half of award-nominated comedy duo BEARD.

Sam Steiner (Writer)

Sam is a playwright and screenwriter from Manchester. His debut play, the award-wining *Lemons Lemons Lemons Lemons Lemons,* was first produced by Walrus, and has subsequently been seen all over the world, in eight different languages. Sam's recent work on stage includes *You Stupid Darkness!* (Paines Plough/Theatre Royal Plymouth) and *Kanye The First* (HighTide).

Other pieces of Sam's work have been showcased at the Royal Exchange, Soho, Southwark Playhouse, Sala Beckett in Barcelona, and the Cannes and London Film Festivals. He completed an attachment at Paines Plough as their Playwright Fellow and holds an MA in Screenwriting from the National Film and Television School.

Sam is currently under commission at Paines Plough, and is developing a television project with Euston North, and a film project with Sunny March. He is a co-founder of Walrus.

Christopher Worrall (Casting Consultant)

As casting director: *If Not Now When* (National Theatre); *Chicken Soup* (Sheffield Crucible); *LAVA* (Nottingham Playhouse).

As associate/assistant: *A Very Expensive Poison, All My Sons, The American Clock, A Christmas Carol* (Old Vic); *Measure for Measure, Aristocrats, The Prime of Miss Jean Brodie, The Way of the World, The York Realist, Belleville, The Lady from the Sea, Committee* (Donmar Warehouse); *Company* (Gielgud).

Film credits include: *Emma* (Working Title).

A TABLE TENNIS PLAY

Sam Steiner

For Ed Madden

'Our weird little mutant play'

Thanks

To the cast and creative team who have inspired, crafted and realised this play with such creativity and delicacy. Beth, Euan and Rosa have as much ownership over these words and characters as I do, and the ingenuity with which the team have achieved this show on a small scale has been a joy to watch.

To Howard Ward and Luke MacGregor for their brilliant guest appearances.

To Ellice Stevens for another wonderful cover design.

To Jess Bray for buying me a beer and reminding me that table tennis is a smaller version of a bigger game.

To Caroline Steiner, the Barley Mow and the town of Hove for a much-needed breath of fresh air.

And to David Prescott and Theatre Royal Plymouth for all their support.

S.S.

'The arena, the card-table, the magic circle, the temple, the stage, the screen, the tennis court, the court of justice, etc., are all in form and function play-grounds, i.e. forbidden spots, isolated, hedged round, hallowed, within which special rules obtain. All are temporary worlds within the ordinary world, dedicated to the performance of an act apart.'

Johan Huizinga, Homo Ludens

'We got one last chance to make it real...'

Bruce Springsteen, 'Thunder Road'

Characters

MIA, *eighteen*
CALLUM, *twenty-nine*
CATH, *thirty-two*

And DAD *and* MAN, *voices off.*

A forward slash (/) indicates the point of interruption in overlapping dialogue.

An en-dash (–) indicates an interruption of speech or train of thought.

Ellipses (…) indicate either a trailing off, a breather or a hesitation.

Punctuation or lack thereof is written to suggest delivery rather than to conform to the rules of grammar.

This text went to press before the end of rehearsals and so may differ slightly from the play as performed.

Notes

An underground World War II air-raid shelter. Buried underneath flowerbeds. Untouched for twenty years. Curved tin plating on the walls. Maybe a drip of water from a pipe. Tons of discarded household items from pre-1990s. Paraphernalia from a dozen different lives. A knackered old table tennis table in the middle of it all. There's a lantern hanging from the ceiling. It would be nice if the play was entirely lit by this lantern, and light coming in from the door (when it's open).

When the door is open we should be able to hear sound from outside. This can be literal or figurative. When it is closed it should be silent.

In the original production all of the clutter, with a couple of noted exceptions, was represented by thousands of table tennis balls. The script has been written to take advantage of that.

Mia always wears her tennis whites and carries an enormous tennis bag on her back – it looks like she could overbalance at any second. Except in the final scene.

Maybe the stage gets progressively clearer as the play goes on.

Maybe scene changes are really quick. A buzz and a flicker. Like the next scene is interrupting the previous one. A shunt forward in time.

BEFORE

When the audience have taken their seats, the stage is plunged into darkness.

Quiet for a few moments.

Eventually we hear the sound of digging. And an old man's muttering. Unintelligible. It's coming from above us. It sounds as if someone is walking on the floor above the ceiling of the theatre.

The sound of a shovel hitting metal. Clanging against it.

The sound of a car pulling up.

More muttering.

From above:

MIA (*from far away*). Dad what are you... come on Dad you should be inside.

DAD (*off*). something. something here.

MIA. What are you doing out – come on

DAD (*off*). something under the flowers.

MIA. There's – what's... what's that?

Sound of a foot on the metal roof.

DAD (*off*). careful there. got to be careful. important. big match coming. ball throw too high for wind last time. yes. hanging left. concentration is the... yes too much. too much going on to... yes. Mia? Mia?

Sound of two feet walking along the roof.

Sound of someone gripping the handle.

Metal scratching against metal as the door opens.

Blast of light and sound for a moment.

Then it settles down to blackness.

MIA *enters shining her phone-torch.*

She's wearing her tennis whites.

(*Off.*) cave. little cave in the garden. hiding in the garden. under the flowers.

safe from the angry angry angry… what was it? in my head? no. yes.

smelly down there.

angry what was it?

bombs. falling from the sky. like fruit.

SATURDAY

Scene One

CATH *and* CALLUM *are sat sorting through the clutter.*
The door is closed. They use torches to look through the clutter.
It's incredibly hot. They occasionally fan themselves/wipe their
foreheads.

Sound of a fly buzzing around. They're looking around for it.

It stops.

Pause.

CALLUM. Uh.

I dunno.

Twenty-nine years.

Three months

And like a week and a half? Ish?

Nine…?

yeah, nine days.

Do you know like your *exact*…?

CATH. Yeah!

CALLUM. Seriously? You know the exact time you were born.

CATH. Mmhmm. So I am – it's what – twelve thirty-three now.
So I am thirty-two years, four months, twelve days, twenty-
one hours and forty-seven minutes old.

CALLUM. WHAT? STOP IT.

CATH. Give or take the seconds.

CALLUM. How do you / know that?

CATH. They don't put seconds on birth certificates.

CALLUM. That's freaky. And also like very impressive mental maths.

CATH. But I guess, if you were gonna put seconds on the clock, do you go from when you're crowning or when you're like fully outta / there?

CALLUM. Are you advocating for like a vaginal photo finish?

CATH. That is what I am advocating for, Callum, yes.

CALLUM. What were you again?

CATH. Uh… thirty-two years, four months, twelve days, twenty-one hours and forty-*eight* minutes old.

CALLUM. Give or take the seconds.

CATH. / Mmhmm.

The fly buzzes again. They look up.

CALLUM. That's gonna get me.

Beat. The buzzing comes in and out for the rest of the scene.

Seven names for bugs?

CATH. Haven't we done bugs before?

CALLUM. I'll check the list.

CALLUM *gets out his phone.*

CATH. Nah I don't feel like playing.

He puts his phone away.

Pause. They sort.

CALLUM. This place makes me itchy.

Like it actually makes me itchy.

Beat.

Like I keep fucking scratching.

Why d'your family even have an air-raid shelter anyway? This far in the country.

CATH. Apparently they were just super-paranoid and my great-granddad was convinced the Germans were like targeting him specifically – (*In a voice:*) HITLER'S AFTER MY DAIRY FAAAAAARM!

The word 'farm' echoes around the space.

CATH *looks around in awe.*

CALLUM *shivers.*

If I had a house I think I'd just fill the whole thing with this kinda stuff.

CALLUM. Yeah? Old broken crap from thirty years ago?

CATH. And I'd never go outside.

CALLUM. People *bought* all this stuff.

Like people actually *bought* and *ohhhhhwned* all this stuff.

Imagine being like:

He picks up a table tennis ball.

Oh here's a tiny wooden bow-and-arrow set – this is worthy of purchase.

CATH. Lemme see that.

He passes her the ball.

She looks at it.

CALLUM. Like… *imagine.*

Does it have to be old stuff like this? We could get a pet or something. That'd be a pretty big change.

CATH. A pet?

CALLUM. Yeah.

CATH. You hate animals.

CALLUM. I love animals. Animals are like… my thing.

CATH. You have allergies. You get rashes.

CALLUM. I was reading this article and apparently there are like herbal remedies you can... Like there are these little pills with tiny bits of cat hair / in them

CATH. You *transform* into a / ... super-powered...

CALLUM. This place gives me the creeps.

CATH. They put hair *in* the pills?

CALLUM. Uh yeah. Apparently.

CATH. Like they pluck the cat and then they stick the hair in the pill and sell it?

CALLUM. I think there are other things in the pill too.

CATH. Danny's got a cat. You could eat some of his hair if you wanna eat some cat.

CALLUM. I'm not gonna eat Danny's cat's hair.

CATH. You should eat some of Danny's cat.

CALLUM. I don't even like Danny. Danny's favourite song is a Bond theme.

CATH. I'm just trying to save you money.

CALLUM. Well I'm just / trying to...

CATH. The cat's name's Oscar by the way, after the awards.

CALLUM. I'm just trying.

Beat.

CATH. Yeah.

CALLUM. i'm here aren't i.

CATH (*maybe awkwardly feeling his face*). You are here.

CALLUM. And I'm sorting the stuff.

CATH. You are sorting the stuff like a fucking pro, Callum.

CALLUM. Thank you.

CATH. I'm serious. You could like... sort stuff in the big leagues.

CALLUM. You're never serious.

CATH *stands up.*

Beat.

You've stood.

CATH *ignores him and begins sticking labels onto the boxes.*

Wait you brought labels?

CATH. Mmhmm.

CALLUM. *You* brought labels.

CATH. Yeah. I thought they'd be useful?

CALLUM. You're someone that brings labels now?

Beat.

CATH. I could be someone that brings labels.

MIA *opens the door. A blast of sound and light that then settles down to the low rumble of the outside world.*

CATH. Hey.   CALLUM. Hiya.

MIA. Hey.

Uh. Would you guys mind if you kept the door open?

CATH. Oh yeah! God, sorry. I just wanted to –

CALLUM. Sorry. Yeah I told her it was fucking batshit / to close that thing but

CATH. I have this thing about small dark spaces. They make me feel all: mmmmm.

CALLUM. It reminds her of the womb.

CATH. Callum likes to psychoanalyse me.

CALLUM. Cath likes to make pillow dens on weekends.

The fly starts buzzing again.

CATH. It's so loud outside. That bypass is new you know – that wasn't there when I lived here. It must've really… affected your… what?

CALLUM *is signalling to* CATH *to stop talking. He has spotted the fly land in the middle of the table tennis table.*

CALLUM (*hushed*). fly.

He downs the liquid from his keep cup.

Slowly approaches the fly.

Slams down the keep cup.

COME ON

CATH. You got it!?

CALLUM. I did.

CATH. You just caught a fly with your keep cup.

CALLUM. I just caught a fly with a keep cup.

CATH. You are a big big man.

CALLUM. I AM A TAMER OF BEASTS.

Beat. MIA *is slightly taken aback by how quickly they speak.*

MIA. Wow that was um…

But with the door…

It's just – while you're / on our like… property…

CATH. Oh god / yeah!

CALLUM. Yeah. Door stays open.

CATH. Wide.

CALLUM. Yeah.

CATH. Open.

MIA. Thanks.

Pause.

I don't mean to be like…

CATH. No!   CALLUM. Not at all.

MIA. You just have to be careful don't you.

CALLUM. Totally. Oh, is there any chance we could get a fan in here?

CATH. Oh – a fan would be amazing actually. / We're sweating our

MIA. Yeah they said it was gonna get really hot before all the rain starts.

CALLUM. Storm Helen.

MIA. Yeah.

CATH. Isn't it Hannah? Storm Hannah.

CALLUM. Pretty sure it's Helen right?

MIA. Errr. I think it's Helen.

CATH. Oh.

MIA. Yeah.

Beat.

I think we've got a fan in the house but it sticks to the left.

CALLUM. That's / fine.

MIA. Like it'll rotate a bit then get stuck on the left-hand side.

CALLUM. Cool.

MIA. I've got a match this afternoon but um Raymond said he'd stick around all day and check on you every hour or so. In case you need anything else or…

CALLUM. Raymond's your dad's / nurse?

MIA. Yeah. He's nice.

They smile at her.

CATH. We should…

CALLUM. Yep.

They return to the sorting.

MIA. Do you uh… do you guys live in London?

CATH. Mmhmm   CALLUM. Yep.

Beat.

MIA (*an understatement*). That's really cool.

I uh... My friend...

She changes her mind.

I've never been.

CALLUM *smiles at her.*

CATH. Cal. Spot.

CALLUM. Argh. Where?

CATH. By your... Can I?

CALLUM. Maybe later.

CALLUM *picks up a ball and shows it to* CATH.

CATH *smiles, laughs a little.*

MIA (*re: the ball*). What's that?

CATH. What?

MIA. The...

CATH. Oh it's a tea cosy?

MIA. Oh. Okay.

Cool.

Scene Two

MIA *appears behind* CATH, *carrying a fan. She has a bit of blood on her top.*

CATH *glances over her shoulder.*

CATH. OH SHIT!

MIA. Oh I'm so sorry / I'm so sorry

CATH. Fuck me. You / terrified the –

MIA. I knew that was gonna happen / and I really didn't wanna scare you.

CATH. It's fine it's fine it's fine. Just…

    CATH *does some deep breathing.*

MIA. I got you a fan.

    She finds a mains plug, maybe on a long extension cable? Or a mini-generator? Turns the fan on and it starts blowing.

CATH. Thanks. How was your – what's on your top?

MIA. Oh um well in the last shot of the game I played a volley that kind of hit the other girl in the face. And then when we were doing the handshake she sneezed and loads of um… yeah.

CATH. Oh god is she okay?

MIA. I think so.

    Beat.

    So tomorrow there's gonna be a little party in the garden

    She nods upwards.

CATH. Oh. Is it a birthday or…?

MIA. It's a victory party.

CATH. Oh. You won!

MIA. Yeah. So it might be a bit loud.

CATH. That's okay. Drunk, horny teenagers are like my spirit animal.

MIA. Oh uh. There won't be any…

It's just like… My coaching team. So…

CATH. Oh. Okay.

Pause.

MIA. Where's um…

CATH. Oh Callum. He had to take a work call.

MIA. On a Saturday?

CATH. Yeah he works for this software company and there's like a big fair on today or something. He was supposed to go but I dragged him up here instead.

MIA. That's nice.

CATH. Yeah well…

He's trying to –

no it is nice.

Pause.

MIA. Do you want some water or anything?

CATH. Oh. I think / I'm

MIA. There's some coconut water in the fridge. It's rich in potassium. If you're… I don't know what your potassium levels are like but it's um… it's pretty good.

CATH. I've got a bottle in the car

MIA. Oh of / coconut or…?

CATH. Just the normal… *Spring?* I think it's from a spring.

MIA. Oh. Cool.

Beat.

CATH. Are you like a – like a *professional* tennis player?

MIA. Um well I dunno what actually / counts as

CATH. Do you make money / from

MIA. Well if I win.

CATH. But like proper money money?

MIA. I mean it's pretty good if you win.

CATH. whoa.

MIA. And like I get a bit from my sponsorship deal even if I lose. Enough for Raymond.

CATH. Your / *sponsorship*

MIA. It's just a little brand. It's not like… I dunno… Adidas or

CATH. Wait, have you like – have you been to Wimbledon?

Beat.

MIA. Uh. No. I mean. I have yeah but not the… just the juniors.

CATH. You've played at fucking Wimbledon!?

MIA.…yeah. I join the tour in a couple of weeks. If I win the next two games.

CATH. You know those towels they use – do you get to keep them afterwards? Or they just wash 'em and use 'em for the next people?

MIA. Yeah / you

CATH. I just always wonder about that.

MIA. You get to keep them yeah.

CATH. So you've just… got some. Lying about.

MIA. Somewhere in the house yeah.

CATH. Wow.

   CATH *looks at everything around her.*

   She puts a hand on the table tennis table.

   Pause.

MIA. Do you play tennis?

CATH. Oh. Uh. No. I took – I'm a nanny for this little boy. Zak. He's Callum's nephew actually. And I took him once but we play all kinds of games so it doesn't really count.

Beat.

What?

MIA. Nothing.

CATH. What?

MIA. It's just weird hearing you call it a… *game*.

CATH. Why?

MIA. I dunno.

Pause.

CATH. I uh… I paint as well though.

MIA. What?

CATH. I do paintings? I'm uh… I'm an artist I guess.

MIA. Wow really?

CATH. Yeah. I hate that word but / yeah.

MIA. What are your paintings of?

CATH. Uh. Mainly just little things. I go to these flea markets and pick up like… really cool old clocks or um I got these little china ramekins with two kind of orange swooshes down them? Apparently they were from Switzerland.

MIA. Wow that's really cool.

CATH. Yeah and this guy in Aberdeen sends me photos of his kids and pays me a hundred pounds to like turn them into paintings. So it's… you know… I get *money* for…

MIA. Yeah.

Uh. That's great.

CATH. Yeah. I tried to – one time – I tried to do a… a landscape? Callum drove me out to the Brecon Beacons in Wales? And we hiked up this hill with a big thirty-by-forty canvas. Sat up there for a few hours.

It was this beautiful kinda… the sunlight was like…

(*Like it's not a big deal*.) but I didn't really know where to start.

Beat.

MIA. Yeah. No. Yeah. That must be really hard.

A weird pause.

CATH. Zak didn't like it when we played.

MIA. Oh.

CATH. Tennis. Not for him I think. He's more of a free spirit probably. Like sometimes we play this game called Seven Things. You know that one? He loves it.

MIA *shakes her head.*

So I go: Give me seven… names for trolls.

Beat. CATH *nods at* MIA.

MIA. Oh uh… But I don't like… I don't know any trolls.

CATH. Yeah you make them up. That's the whole… thing.

MIA. My imagination isn't very good. I'm not a – what did you call Zak?

CATH. Just do it!

Beat.

MIA. Does it have to be the troll thing? Like is it always about trolls?

CATH *laughs.*

CATH. No. It's not always trolls. Uh. Okay give me seven… types of cloud.

MIA. Uh. Okay. Um.

I think there's some called… Cumulus.

CATH. Cumulus. One.

MIA. Ssssss… sirus? Cirrus.

CATH. Cirrus. Two.

MIA. Oh and then there's uh… it's like a combination… cumu-cirro – cirrocumulus.

CATH. Cirrocumulus. Three. Very impressive knowledge of clouds.

MIA. Um. Ohhhhhh.

CATH. No hesitating. Come on!

MIA. I don't know / any more.

CATH. Make them up!

MIA. I don't – I can't

CATH. Come on!

CATH *starts banging the table tennis table rhythmically.*

MIA. Um. Oh. Okay. Uh. Table-mulus.

CATH. Table-mulus! Great. Four.

MIA. Um cup… Cup. Cuppy.

CATH. CUPCUPCUPPY. FIVE.

MIA. Uh. Wow. Okay.

CATH. Two more.

MIA. Lon… doniferous.

CATH. Londoniferous! One more.

MIA *looks at* CATH.

MIA. You.

Uh. You…

Youyou.

CATH. Youyou?

MIA.…yeah.

CATH. THAT IS SEVEN THINGS!

MIA (*VERY relieved*). Oh. Uh. Whoa. Great.

CATH. Good game right.

MIA (*nodding a lot*). Yeah.

Yeah.

CATH. Fun.

Pause.

CATH *looks at* MIA, *concerned.*

Well um… we can play ping pong now if you want?

MIA. Oh uh.

CATH. You must like… know all the *spins*?

MIA *giggles.*

'All the spins'

MIA. No it's… I don't know anyone who doesn't play tennis so it's… cool.

CATH *serves the ball in.*

MIA *just stands there.*

CATH. What?

MIA.…it's stupid.

CATH. What is?

MIA. I don't really play ping pong.

CATH. What? Why?

MIA. It's just like a… superstition thing.

CATH. I don't get it.

MIA. That if I like – oh it's so stupid.

Pause. MIA *looks down.*

That if I play… (*Nods at the table.*)

I'll mess up my tennis.

MIA *nods.*

CATH. That's fucking ridiculous!

MIA. I know.

CATH. You're a crazy woman.

> CATH *serves the ball in.*

> MIA *doesn't move.*

> *Pause.*

> CALLUM *enters.*

CALLUM. Sorry about that.

CATH. Cal play with me!

> CALLUM *casually picks up a bat and they immediately start to rally.*

> *As they play* MIA *slinks away. She picks up one of the table tennis balls – maybe the one that is a tea cosy – and stares at it really hard, trying to see it.*

> Imagine if we lift the mug up later and there's like a different animal under there.

CALLUM. What?

CATH. Like it's evolved or / transformed.

MIA. Changed?

CATH. Yeah.

CALLUM (*affectionately*). You're a fucking weirdo.

> So Stevie and Pav are panicking a bit. People aren't really stopping at the stall and they're stressed about the keynote.

CATH. I'm sorry you're not there.

CALLUM. No – I wasn't trying to guilt-trip…

CATH. I didn't think you were.

CALLUM. Cool.

CATH. Did you whack out The Voice to calm them down?

CALLUM. Uh I mean I spoke to them in / like a normal register.

CATH. Callum has this thing he does where he just kind of lowers and softens his voice so you have to like lean in to hear what he's saying. And it's bizarrely soothing. Like the rest of the – wherever you are – goes blurry.

CALLUM. It's not like a *thing*. I just speak quieter sometimes?

CATH. COME TO ME AND LET ME EMOTIONALLY MANIPULATE / YOU WITH MY VELVETY VOICEBOX.

CALLUM. Whoa that's… okay…? I'm not trying to… / emotionally manipulate

CATH. No I love it. I LOVE it. Do it for Mia.

CALLUM. I'm not gonna do it for Mia. I don't even know what *it* is.

CATH. Do it for Mia!

Beat.

CALLUM. We should um…

CATH. What time / is it?

CALLUM. Oh crap Mia. I'm so sorry but I – I was just like walking around and there was a little glass bottle outside your front door and well I knocked it over and it uh… shattered.

MIA. Oh no.

CALLUM. I couldn't tell what was in it? It was unbranded.

Beat.

MIA. It's okay.

CATH. Are you sure?

MIA. Yeah it's fine.

My dad used to be really in to whisky and this uh… this guy in Scotland sends him nice bottles every now and then. / But it's okay.

CALLUM. Oh my god.   CATH. Okay shit we'll – can
                                      we replace it?

MIA. It's okay. He can't really drink it any more. It's no big deal.

Beat.

What time is it?

CALLUM. Just gone eight.

CATH. Oh wow. When did /   MIA. No it's not.
that happen?

CALLUM. Uh… yeah it is?

MIA (*hurrying to door*). Nonono/nononono

CALLUM. Everything okay?   CATH. What's…?

MIA. My dad just has to take his pills at really specific – I'll be
right back

She leaves.

CATH *and* CALLUM *share a look like: bless her.*

CALLUM. We should get back to the B&B.

CATH. Yeah.

CALLUM. They're saying they might have to close the roads if
the rain starts tonight.

CATH. Yeah. You know those towels they use at Wimbledon?

CALLUM. Uh. Yeah?

CATH. They get to keep them. Like take them home, put 'em up.

CALLUM.…okay?

Why did you have to like… say that about my quiet-voice
thing?

CATH. Say what?

CALLUM. What you said.

CATH. What did I say. That I fricking love it?

CALLUM. Well it was like, the *way* you were saying it.

CATH. Cal I adore The Voice

CALLUM. I know you do / it's just

CATH. It's like birdsong to me.

CALLUM. Well now you're being –

CATH. What?

CALLUM. Sarcastic.

CATH. I'm not. Genuinely. I would rather listen to you
speaking in The Voice than birds singing.

CALLUM. I can't tell if you're

CATH. What?

CALLUM. I dunno. I'm just confused.

Beat.

CATH. Did you use your The Voice on *Alison*?

CALLUM. No I didn't use it on Alison.

CATH. You didn't like *serenade* her with it / beforehand.

CALLUM. No I didn't *serenade* / her with it.

CATH. Does she have a pet too – is that why you wanna take
those cat pills?

CALLUM. No!

Yes. She has a tortoise.

CATH. She has a fucking tortoise?

CALLUM. yeah.

CATH. Wait was it like In The Room when you guys

CALLUM. No. Fuck no. Jesus.

CATH. So just the two of you then?

Pause.

Eurghhhhhh. I just saw that from the outside and I really hate
myself – so let's just / parallel universe…

CALLUM. I don't know *why* I –

That thing at Jeanie's really fucked me up.

CATH. I know. Let's not – let's talk about something else. Serve the ball.

CALLUM. I didn't even like Alison, you know. Like she's mean. She's really mean.

CATH. You've said.

CALLUM. She stole a fiver out of my wallet and she laughed at this disabled guy on the street.

Plus I think she's probably an alcoholic

Not like a 'Hi, I'm an an Alcoholic' alcoholic.

But sometimes she'd have like eleven vodka tonics on a Tuesday.

You don't wanna…

CATH. No it's… I don't know why I keep… I'm not angry at all. Like genuinely I don't feel anger / inside me.

CALLUM. No Cath it's cool to still be angry. Like it's *very understandable* that you're angry.

CATH. But I'm not.

Pause.

MIA *enters*.

MIA. Hey. Sorry.

CATH. Hey! Uh. We were just saying that we should get back to the B&B in case the uh… Storm Hannah / hits

CALLUM. Helen.

CATH. Helen.

MIA. Oh uh. Yeah of course.

CATH. But thanks for having us! I think we made a great start!

MIA. Okay.

They pack up.

CALLUM *heads for the exit*.

CALLUM. So nice to meet you, Mia.

MIA. Yeah. See you tomorrow.

CALLUM exits.

CATH follows.

As she's about to go:

It's cool to see you again.

CATH. Yeah.

Sorry have we… met before?

MIA. Oh uh. I thought maybe when my family came to look round the house?

Maybe not though. / I'm probably

CATH. You must have been tiny!

MIA. Yeah. I dunno why I thought…

Beat.

You were dancing in the garden.

CATH looks at her.

Pause.

CATH. My mum died in this room.

MIA. What!?

CATH. Yeah. I… Sorry I don't know why I said that. I just wanted to… I dunno…

She waves her arms as if to say: put it out there.

MIA. She died in this room?

CATH. Yeah! That's weird isn't it.

Beat.

MIA. How?

CATH. She had like a pulmonary… just dropped dead.

MIA. Whoa. How… how old was she?

Pause.

CATH. Thirty-two years, four months, fifteen days, nine hours and thirty-eight minutes old.

CALLUM (*from off*). Cath?

CATH. YEP yep.

(*To* MIA.) Uh don't mention it to – it freaks him out when we talk / about

CALLUM *enters*.

Hey.

CALLUM. We should… I don't wanna speed down all those roads. I'll get carsick.

They exit.

They're offstage by now. We can maybe hear a murmured conversation by the car.

The stage is empty.

Sound of the car driving off.

Silence.

Suddenly the keep cup on the table begins to rattle. Of its own accord.

It's just slight at first.

But begins to grow louder and more aggressive.

MIA *enters*.

She stares at it, paralysed.

She steps towards it.

Then stops.

Then moves closer.

It's rattling harder and harder.

It's terrifying.

Maybe the lights begin to flicker.

She takes a deep breath.

She grabs the cup and lifts it up.

A sparrow flies out of it, into the audience.

SUNDAY

Scene One

CATH *is sorting more quickly and energetically than before.*
MIA *stood behind.*

We watch her for a while. She is trying to be very organised.

Long silence as she sorts.

MIA. Wow you're uh… you're going really fast.

CATH. Yep.

MIA. Where's Callum?

CATH. Oh um… he decided he had to go to the fair today.

MIA. Oh no. Really?

CATH. Yeah.

MIA. Is he coming back or…?

CATH. Not sure.

No, it depends on the roads and stuff.

MIA. Oh okay.

Pause.

When I came down this morning there were these heat shimmers coming off the table.

CATH. Really?

MIA. Yeah it felt like something was gonna explode… you can kinda… if you crouch and squint.

MIA *crouches down and squints, looking at the table.*

CATH *stops sorting and does the same.*

Can you…?

CATH. Uh…

Pause. CATH *doesn't see them.*

MIA. They're not really there   CATH. Oh… yeah.
any more.

An embarrassed pause.

Then CATH *resumes sorting.*

We hear distant chants of: 'MIA MIA MIA MIA' from the garden above.

CATH. Do you need to get back to your…

MIA. It's winding down.

If you want to come up for a bit you can?

CATH. Thanks. I should probably / get on

MIA. There might be like a lot of tennis chat –

CATH. I can understand tennis chat.

Beat.

MIA. Yeah I… I wasn't saying you couldn't.

I just thought you might find it boring.

CATH. Oh okay.

Pause.

MIA. Or I could help you down here?

CATH. There's like a *really* complicated sorting system so…

MIA. What is it?

Beat.

CATH. Uh. So it's… red labels for rubbish. Green for stuff to keep. And orange for stuff I'm not sure about yet.

MIA. Like a Maybe box?

CATH. Uh… sure.

MIA. Okay.

CATH. That's a uh… that's a big crown.

MIA (*taking it off*).…yeah. Uh. They made me wear it.

CATH. Right. No it suits you.

MIA. Do you think?

CATH. Yeah. You should wear it all the time. Crowns rock.

MIA. Thanks.

Beat.

Thanks.

MIA *tentatively goes to join the sorting.*

She sits near CATH.

Pause.

What's that?

She points at one of the piles.

CATH. Oh…

CATH *pulls an actual record player out from amongst the table tennis balls.*

MIA. wow.

CATH *heaves it onto the table.*

There's a record on it.

CATH (*reading*). *Bruce Springsteen Live 1975–85.*

MIA. Oh cool.

CATH. You like that one?

MIA. Yeah.

I mean.

I don't really know it.

Beat. The chants from the garden have started up again.

Do you wanna like… try it out?

CATH. What?

MIA. Let's try it out.

CATH. Nah / let's…

   MIA *goes to try the record player.*

   (*Very firmly.*) No.

   Beat.

   It just might not work so there's… there's like no point.

   Beat.

MIA. Okay yeah. No you're right.

   CATH *wipes her forehead and returns to sorting.*

   MIA *watches.*

   Pause.

   Do you like whisky?

CATH. Um. I guess?

   MIA *grins.*

MIA. Okayokayokayokayokayokay.

   MIA *runs out.*

   CATH *looks after her, amused.*

   She closes the record player and tries to resume sorting.

   MIA *runs back in carrying a load of bottles of whisky.*

CATH. Whoa.

MIA. It's a lot.

CATH. Yeah.

MIA. A tasting game! So – so my dad / collects –

CATH. You said.

MIA. And um whisky takes years and years and years to brew. Ferment.

CATH. Right.

MIA. So I was trying to think of um games that we could –
yeah – and I thought we could uh… you could taste the
whisky and try to guess which year it came from?

Beat.

CATH. Uh. I'm really trying to be focused, Mia.

MIA. I just thought it might be fun. We'll play best of three?

Pause. CATH *sighs.*

CATH. Okay.

MIA *puts the shot glasses down and pours three shots of
whisky.*

She gives the first to CATH.

CATH *weighs it up.*

CATH *has a tiny sip of the first.*

She winces.

Wow.

MIA. Are you gonna… finish the…

CATH. I'm good.

MIA. Okay well how old do you…

CATH. I have no idea.

MIA. You have to guess.

CATH. um. (*Old voice.*) Two hundred years!

Pause.

MIA. It's seven but…

CATH. Oh. Okay. Sorry for – I hate it when people do that.
Undermine your impressive / story.

MIA. Next one!

CATH (*eyebrows raised*). OKAY THEN.

MIA. Unless… would this be more fun if we wait for Callum?

CATH. Uh. Why?

MIA. I dunno.

CATH. Do you find him attractive?

MIA. Whoa. Uh…

I don't know what you want me to say to that.

CATH. I don't want you to say anything.

MIA. Well I don't know what to say then.

CATH. Do you only say things that you think people want you to say?

MIA. No.

Beat.

I think you two are like the best couple I've ever seen.

CATH. Really?

MIA. Yeah it's like… yeah. Definitely. You guys are like magic.

Beat.

CATH. That's funny.

MIA. Why?

CATH. No that's really nice. I'll tell him. That's really nice.

Pause.

They look at each other.

CATH *smiles.*

CATH *sips the next shot. Winces again.*

Um it's stronger? Say seventeen.

MIA. Eighteen!

CATH. What. Seriously?

MIA. Yeah!

CATH. I won?

MIA. You won.

Beat.

CATH. Well. Shit.

I'm a winner.

MIA. Yeah.

CATH. I'm someone that wins.

CATH downs the rest of the shot.

Winces.

Okay as a victory prize / can I

MIA. Oh uh. We didn't say we were doing victory…

CATH. No but just –

MIA. You have to keep the same rules. Otherwise it's not a game it's / just… normal life.

CATH. Just let me pop those three little spots you've got on your forehead.

MIA shrinks away self-consciously.

Come on.

I'm really good and really gentle.

Pause.

MIA. Okay.

CATH goes over to MIA. They kneel opposite each other.

CATH brushes MIA's hair behind her ears.

CATH starts to squeeze the first spot.

Pause. Eventually:

Nearlytherenearlytherenearlythere.

Aaaaaaaaaand there we go!

Pause. MIA draws away.

She puts her finger where the spot was.

CATH. Look I've got your pus on my hand.

MIA. Oh my god that's so gross. I'm sorry.

CATH. Why are you sorry?

CATH wipes it on her jeans.

Two more?

Beat.

MIA *nods.*

They move back together.

MIA. Did your mum used to do this for you?

CATH. My brother did for a bit. Till I got *The Taste*.

You? Probably like your doubles partner or something right?

MIA *goes to shake her head.*

Staaaaay still.

MIA. Sorry.

Pause.

She lives in London now.

CATH. Who?

MIA. My doubles partner. She moved.

CATH. Oh whereabouts?

MIA. Um. The – (*Wincing.*) S-OWWW/WWWWTH I think.

CATH. sorrysorrysorrysorry

CATH lifts off. MIA rubs the spot a bit.

CATH goes back in.

Pause.

MIA. Is that near where you and Callum live?

CATH. No. Not really.

What was her name?

Beat.

(*As if* MIA *hadn't heard her.*) What was / her name?

MIA. Do you mind if I don't tell you?

CATH pulls back for a moment. Brushes more hair out of MIA's eyes. Smiles at her sadly.

MIA tilts her head so the spot is towards CATH.

CATH places the palm of her hand over MIA's whole face.

Er...?

CATH (*laughing*). Sorry!

She pulls away.

My mum used to do that to me – just put her palm over my face. Whenever I'd like grazed my knee, or was throwing some sort of strop. I always thought it must look so weird from the outside.

CATH goes in one last time and pops the last spot.

Pause.

Zak's mum – Callum's sister, a while ago she met this guy who lived in America, in Boston I think and decided to er, to run off with him basically. So she's packing her bags and Ben, the dad, is just throwing everything she packs out of the bag and shouting. Clothes flying everywhere, like we're inside a tumble dryer. And um – out of the back door – slidey-glass-door-window thing I see Zak has set up all the garden chairs in a row and he's sat at the front of them. He loves trains. Crazy about trains. So I run out to him, down the row of chairs, and I kind of smother him, pick him up and he just looks up at me and says: 'Don't hug the engine, Cath, or the carriages won't think it's real.'

Don't hug the engine or the carriages won't think it's real.

He'd imagined it and thus, it was.

So I put him back down and he tries to uh... to get back inside it – scrunches his little face up.

But he's, you know...

He's lost the trust of the carriages.

God this one's a real...

She pauses and concentrates on the spot.

She squeezes a bit too hard.

MIA. ah.

CATH. That felt like the *cruellest* thing.

Taking him out of –

Sorry. Why am I telling you this?

Long pause.

The last spot goes.

There we go!

MIA.…thanks.

CATH. Thank *you*! That was a solid hit.

MIA *grins.*

CATH *spots an unopened bottle.*

How old's that one?

MIA. That one is a hundred and twenty-seven years old.

CATH. What!?

MIA (*proudly*). Mmhmm.

CATH. Fuck! When that was bottled… Queen Victoria was still…

MIA. Yeah.

CATH. The whole world has

MIA. Changed.

CATH. Like a hundred times.

A person in like Tennessee…

MIA. Scotland.

CATH. Yeah in like 1800.

MIA. 1892.

CATH. A person in Scotland in 1892 picked up this bottle, opened it, poured in the whisky, closed it and now it's here.

MIA *nods*.

Are you saving it?

MIA *nods*.

What for?

MIA. When I'm like… old enough I guess.

CATH. You're eighteen though right?

MIA. Mmhmm.

(*Re: whisky shots*.) You've got one more.

CATH *sips the whisky*.

CATH. I like that one. I'll say thirteen.

MIA. Thirty-two.

CATH. Aw crap.

MIA. Just like you.

CATH. What?

MIA. Thirty-two.

CATH. Oh yeah. (*Absent-mindedly*.) How d'you know my age?

She weighs the bottle in her hands.

This is my whole life.

She starts laughing.

MIA *doesn't understand. But starts laughing as well, tentatively.*

MIA. Okay, as a… as *my* victory prize

CATH. Wait you win just cos I got it wrong?

MIA. Can we try out the record player?

Beat.

I really think it might work.

Pause. CATH *considers.*

CATH. Alright.

MIA *grins at her, widely.*

The chants from the garden have started up again. Initially they're the same as before: 'MIA MIA MIA MIA.' Then they get weird.

MIA *goes over to the record player.*

MIA *lowers the needle onto the record.*

They wait.	*Chants from outside:*
	'MIA MIA MIA MIA
	SHE'S THE ONE TO
	TRULY FEAR
	SMASH A BALL INTO
	YOUR HEAD
	TENNIS WHITES ARE
	STAINED WITH RED
Nothing.	*MIA MIA MIA MIA*
	VANISH AND THEN
	REAPPEAR
	UNDERGROUND AND
	OVERHEAD
	HIDE BENEATH THE
	FLOWERBED
CATH *stands and takes over: tries to adjust the needle so it works.*	*MIA MIA MIA MIA*
	BETTER EVERY SINGLE
	YEAR
	SHAKE THE EARTH ON
	WHICH WE TREAD
	SOON WE KNOW WE'LL
	ALL BE DEAD.'

Nothing.

Ah.

The chants get louder and louder.

Pause.

Wow they're really…

CATH *starts sorting again.*

MIA. I'll be right back.

MIA *exits. Cheers from the crowd.*

CATH *on stage alone.*

She sorts.

Suddenly CATH *tips over the box she's sorting. Table tennis balls spill over the stage.*

MIA *re-enters.*

Oh no / what…

CATH. Oh it was… the wind.

MIA. The wind?

CATH. I.

Want…

To play ping pong.

MIA. Well maybe when Callum gets back you guys / can have a

CATH. I want to play ping pong with you.

MIA. Oh. Sorry. I can't.

CATH. Pleeeeeaaase.

CATH *picks up the hundred-and-twenty-seven-year-old bottle of whisky.*

MIA. What are you doing?

CATH. Play with me!

MIA. Can you…

CATH. One game and I'll give it you back. One RALLY.

MIA. Please / can I –

CATH. ONE RALLY COME ON

CATH serves the ball in.

MIA stands still.

CATH serves the ball in again.

She serves it in again.

Pause.

MIA picks up a bat.

She stands at the table waiting.

CATH serves the ball in.

They rally until it goes out of play.

There you go. That wasn't that hard right? That won't have ruined your tennis forever.

MIA. No.

CATH. No?

MIA. I mean yeah it was – it was fun.

Pause.

CATH gives her back the bottle.

thanks.

CATH. Do you uh… d'you wanna play some more or…?

MIA. sure.

She doesn't move.

Pause.

CATH. I'm sorry if I've like offended you or…

MIA. No.

CATH. It feels like I've… like mortally…

MIA forces a smile and shakes her head.

MIA shrinks to her knees.

CATH *edges over to her and kind of slowly and confusedly hugs her.*

As CATH *gets halfway into the hug,* MIA *throws her arms around her and grips her tight.*

CATH *is a bit taken aback.*

CATH *puts a hand on the back of* MIA*'s head.*

MIA. Can we not talk about it.

CATH. Okay.

MIA *pulls away and stands up.*

Pause.

I might go.

MIA. No.

Pause.

I looked up your birthday.

You knew your mum's age down to the minute.

When you told me.

Are you…

Are you about to be that?

To become that.

CATH. That's really personal, Mia.

MIA. I'm sorry.

But you are, aren't you.

Pause.

CATH. That's really fucking personal.

I don't even –

We don't even know each other.

MIA. sorry.

Pause.

When?

sorry. no.

CATH *considers*.

CATH. Tomorrow.

MIA. What time?

CATH. 11.24 p.m.

MIA. whoa.

Pause.

CATH. I wanted to try to… *properly* try to organise her stuff, take it home and like, have it around me when…

MIA. Do you think something's gonna happen?

CATH. I dunno.

Beat.

No fuck it yeah. Why not? Why can't there be this one moment where everything just…

Pause.

MIA. I think you should come here. I don't have to be here. It can be just you.

Cos like… maybe it will?

CATH *stares at her for a moment*.

A sudden rush comes over CATH. *She doubles over*.

CATH. God I feel like I'm gonna…

My chest feels – IT'S SO HOT DOWN HERE.

MIA. Do you want some coconut water?

CATH. Yeah fucking give me the stupid coconut water.

MIA. It's good for potassium.

CATH *sips that potassium-rich coconut water*.

She empties the rest over her head to cool down, breathing heavily.

…it's… really expensive.

CATH *pants*.

You should sit down.

CATH *shakes her head*.

(*VERY authoritatively*.) Sit down and put your head between your legs.

CATH *is a bit taken aback and does what* MIA *says*.

Outside the sound of rain and wind begins.

It starts as a light pattering and then increases to a bluster.

MIA *turns towards the door. She slowly, tentatively moves towards it and closes it.*

For the first time the background noise stops.

Total silence.

Just their breathing.

MIA *goes to sit next to* CATH. *Who has her head between her legs.*

CATH. This is actually very uncomfortable.

MIA *smiles*.

Pause.

MIA. It's so quiet.

CATH *nods*.

Imagine if like… if when we open the door it's been weeks and Storm Helen has come and gone. And all of the tennis courts in England have flooded.

MIA *wipes her eyes to find that she's crying*.

I don't know why.

Beat.

CATH. You don't need to know why.

Pause.

I wish I could play real tennis. Like fully sized tennis.

I think what I'd like is for people to see me playing real tennis.

And go: wow she's… she's really in it.

Silence.

CATH *puts a hand over* MIA*'s foot.*

MONDAY

Scene One

CALLUM *on stage alone.*

He is holding a bottle of whisky in a brown-paper bag.

He puts it down on the table. Picks up a table tennis bat and does some keepie-uppies.

Hail is falling on the roof. Dozens of percussive pings.

Pause.

The door opens.

MIA *enters. She's soaked. Maybe her hair is down for the first time?*

CALLUM. Hey! Was it hailing out there?

MIA. You left the door open?

CALLUM. Oh yeah – I thought you wanted us to?

MIA *closes the door.*

MIA. I think it's starting to.

CALLUM. In August.

CALLUM *shakes his head.*

MIA *goes over to* CALLUM *and kind of side-hugs him.*

He is confused by this.

Uh. I got you this!

He holds out the whisky.

MIA. Oh wow.

CALLUM. So I don't know what type the one that I broke was. But the guy at the shop said this one is really good.

MIA. Oh. Great.

CALLUM. Uh.... Okay. Dun Dun Duh: 'A damp tweed with black pepper, smoky vanilla and ozone notes'!

MIA *smiles*.

How was your party?

MIA. It was okay thanks.

CALLUM. Great.

That's fucking awesome.

Beat.

(*As if the thought has just occurred to him.*) Uh d'you know where Cath is?

MIA. No. I uh... I fell asleep in here. And then she was gone when I woke up.

CALLUM. Wait she came yesterday?

MIA. Yeah?

CALLUM. Oh.

MIA. Oh did she not...

CALLUM. Said she was gonna go see a friend instead. Was Stace here too?

MIA. Uh / who's

CALLUM. Don't worry about it.

Pause.

Can I ask you something?

MIA. Mmhmm.

CALLUM. Did she... when I was on that phone call on Saturday, or yesterday come to think of it... did Cath say something to you?

MIA. Uh

CALLUM. About me.

MIA. Oh. Um. Yes! She did!

CALLUM. What uh… what did she say?

MIA. I said that you were the best couple I'd ever met. And she agreed.

MIA *beams at him*.

CALLUM. Uh. Really?

MIA. Yeah. She said she couldn't wait to tell you.

Beat.

CALLUM. That doesn't really… sound like her.

MIA. Well that's what she said.

Pause.

CALLUM. Do you have a boyfriend, Mia? – girlfriend?

MIA. …not really. There's someone that I… you know… sometimes.

CALLUM. Oh. Okay.

Beat.

MIA. He's my tennis coach. / Well, assistant coach.

CALLUM. Oh. Is that like…

Is that… okay?

MIA. Oh yeah. It was my idea.

But we don't really –

(*Proudly*.) We're a secret.

Pause.

CALLUM. Well um. Okay then. If you're sure you're not being…

MIA. I'm not.

CALLUM. I feel kinda uncomfortable now.

MIA *shakes her head*.

Why did you just tell me that?

Beat.

MIA. I don't know.

I thought… But now that you're asking I feel like… like I've done something weird.

CALLUM. No.

Beat.

MIA. How did the fair go?

CALLUM. Uh. I mean I heard it went okay? I was… here though.

MIA. No. Yesterday.

CALLUM. Yesterday I went home.

MIA. Oh. Why?

CALLUM. She told you I went to the fair?

Pause.

MIA. Did you guys have like a… a misunderstanding or something?

CALLUM. Errr no. It's… It was my fault.

Beat.

Sorry I don't mean to… How's your um – Cath was saying that you're gearing up for the tour?

MIA. Oh uh – that's nice that she…

Yeah.

I'm not sure though.

CALLUM. You gotta win the next few games right? To get on – qualify.

MIA. Yeah. I'm considering my options I guess.

CALLUM. She didn't make any plans to like – what time she was gonna…

MIA. Oh well it's the – oh no you don't like to talk about –

CALLUM. What?

MIA. Nothing.

CALLUM. What?

MIA. No it's… She said that you find it all a bit

MIA shivers.

CALLUM. Find what? I don't know what you're talking about, Mia?

Pause.

Mia?

MIA. yeah?

CALLUM. Well – could you… tell me about – please. Whatever was said.

MIA starts organising the boxes even quicker.

I think she just gets ideas in her head sometimes.

Like a few months ago we got a bit high at my friend Jeanie's and – there was a group of us – and Cath just tells the whole crowd that like the way she feels emotions is 'smaller' than the way I feel emotions. More contained. So like she'll never love me as much as I love her. This is in front of all my friends from school. Who I hadn't seen in like a year.

It's just weird behaviour.

Like: *weird*.

And even if that's *true* then I feel like bad for her, you know?

Beat. MIA doesn't respond.

You know what I mean? Like that's sad.

CALLUM stares really intensely at MIA.

MIA. Yeah it's sad.

CALLUM. Right?

She nods.

Beat.

It's weird that I'm here isn't it.

MIA. No it's nice.

CALLUM. You're very polite / but really you don't have to…

MIA. No honestly it's really cool. You can come / whenever you want to –

CALLUM. No Mia I am a fucking nutjob!

Pause.

Did you ever have like a perfect haircut?

MIA. What?

CALLUM. Like did you ever have a haircut where you're like this – *this* – is the best haircut I've ever had. This is the best my hair *has* or *will* ever look. I deeply love this haircut. And like every haircut since then is just you fucking desperately trying to get back to *that* – to, to recreate how that felt, right?

Beat.

MIA. Uh. Well I just go back to the same person.

CALLUM. Yeah! Yeah! Exactly! But that doesn't work! That's my point. Cos like –

MIA. Her name's Barbara. She's really good.

CALLUM. Ah.

Pause. CALLUM *stands there, shaking his head.*

MIA *speaks quietly and genuinely.*

MIA. i don't understand.

CALLUM. Don't worry.

MIA. what should I have said?

Pause.

what should I have said?

CATH *enters. She's drenched as well.*

CATH. Oh. Hi.

MIA. Hey! Uh. So I thought we could concentrate on the boxes again. And maybe sort some of the of the of the stuff in the

Maybe boxes into the Yes and No boxes. Because right now there's a lot in the Maybe boxes. I think they're probably the most popular boxes actually. Don't you think?

CATH. Um. Yeah. I think you may be right.

CATH walks over to CALLUM, rubs his arm and kisses him on the cheek.

She sits down on the floor and resumes sorting.

CALLUM *just stands there.*

MIA. Oh and I uh… Oh I don't know if you… I made some flapjacks for my dad. But now that I think about it I could make him some more for later so

They've got sultanas in! I don't know how you guys feel about sultanas.

CATH. We LOVE sultanas.

CALLUM. Uh yeah sultanas… rock hard.

MIA. Oh wow! What are the odds!

Pause.

Okay. I'll um… I'll go and get them but I'll come straight back afterwards.

CALLUM. thanks Mia.

CATH (*absent-mindedly*). Thanks Mia!

MIA *exits.*

Long silence. CALLUM *goes to say something but doesn't know what.* CATH *stays focused on the sorting.*

Eventually CALLUM *kneels down and helps* CATH *with the sorting.*

They sort in silence for a while.

CATH *glances at* CALLUM. *Then looks away.*

CALLUM *glances at* CATH. *Then looks away.*

Excited for the flapjacks?

CALLUM *starts laughing.*

CATH *starts laughing as well.*

This builds until they are properly pissing themselves.

Then CATH *starts kissing* CALLUM. *There's a frantic desperation to it.*

Maybe she kisses him all over his head when he starts to pull away.

Maybe she starts trying to undo his belt.

CALLUM. stop.

She doesn't stop.

stop.

She stops.

Gets up quickly.

Goes over to the table tennis table.

CATH. Can we just like... do the parallel-universe thing. It happened in a different universe but not in this one. Cool! Great.

CALLUM. How many parallel universes are full of our fights now?

CATH. Well there are infinite parallel universes Callum. So the tiniest proportion possible. Like effectively, mathematically none of them.

Feel better?

Pause.

Play with me.

Just... rally.

CALLUM. I don't wanna play.

CATH. Just be *here*. It'll be fun. And and and we'll be happy.

CALLUM. Then what?

What happens when we stop playing?

Beat.

CATH (*without believing it*). Everything will be different.

Pause.

He stands.

She serves it in.

They rally.

Pause.

Eventually:

CALLUM. I read our list this morning.

CATH. What list?

CALLUM. The seven-things list.

CATH. You read the whole thing?

CALLUM. Yeah.

CALLUM *gets his phone out. He begins to read them. Soon his voice softens into The Voice. About halfway through, he puts his phone down, resumes rallying and recites them from memory.*

Seven ways to get a bartender's attention. Seven names for cocktails. Seven reasons to go back to yours. Seven new kinds of public transport. Seven historical figures you'd most like to fuck. Seven herbal hangover cures. Seven Matthew McConaughey characters. Seven worst sex positions. Seven best sex positions. Seven excuses for pulling a sickie today. Seven things to put on pasta. Seven games to play with kids. Seven ideas for software pitches. Seven things not to say in front of Phil and Mila. Seven worst lies you've ever told. Seven things you'd most like to paint. Seven cities you'd like to live in. Seven ways to kill my sister so that she's dead and never ever comes back. Seven Eras of Civilisation that last longer than a flight to Boston with stops in Edinburgh and Philadelphia. Seven ways to kidnap a child. Seven kinds of train. Seven things my mum will say within an hour. Seven sexiest things about my dad. Seven types of laughter. Seven photographs you'd save in a literal or non-literal fire. Seven world events that could have happened while we've been playing. Seven kinds of rain. Seven things that would get us thrown out of this airport. Seven 'Frenchie French-French' things. Seven weirdest people to bump into while we're here. Seven ways to cook salmon. Seven colours for the curtains. Seven terrible inventions. Seven ways to calm down. Seven reasons to be afraid. Seven evil villains. Seven cities you'll never live in. Seven ways to pass the time. Seven games to play with kids. Seven reasons I should go to the thing. Seven worse things you could've said in front of all my friends. Seven emotions you'll never feel. Seven ways to get the fuck over yourself. Seven games to play instead. Seven names for post-punk bands. Seven gods of torture. Seven battle cries. Seven fruits you can't juice. Seven ways to be better. Seven kinds of prayer. Seven colours of hair dye. Seven brands of dishwasher tablet. Seven ways she's different. Seven ways to ruin a painting. Seven ideas for trips. Seven ideas for activities. Seven ideas for dates. Seven magic spells. Seven ancient languages. Seven tools for digging in the dirt. Seven things to hide inside. Seven ways to measure time. Seven ways to resurrect the dead. Seven roads that never end. Seven kinds of sunlight.

And seven names for bugs.

Silence.

What are we… just tell me what we're doing here and I'll try to be in it with you. I will. I want to. I love you. And I don't care if that's more than you can… just tell me what we're doing.

MIA *enters with flapjacks. And maybe some kitchen roll. As she does so:*

CATH. We're playing ping pong.

CALLUM *attempts to smash the ball. It feels VERY aggressive. Maybe the lights flicker a bit as he does so.*

Pause.

CALLUM. I'm sorry.

MIA. I haven't cut them up yet. So we're gonna have to tear them with our fingers. I brought some kitchen roll because then our hands won't get too buttery and we won't get butter on all the great stuff in here.

CATH. Thanks Mia!

Pause. CATH *serves the ball back in.* MIA *starts breaking up the flapjacks.*

CALLUM. Cath, I'm sorry. That was aggressive and I didn't mean it to be.

Pause.

I feel like I… attacked you…

CATH. It's okay.

CALLUM. oh god I feel kinda sick.

MIA. Hey do you guys think… I was thinking I might – at some point – I might try to come to London because because I've never been before and um… it's obviously totally cool if you don't have room or anything but if there's any chance I could stay with you guys for like a night or two?

If I don't go on the tour.

I know you must be busy.

You must have lots of people to… to go to the cinema with or…

You guys seem kinda tired.

If you wanna have a nap or…

Cos that would be okay with me?

If you wanted to.

Maybe we should go outside.

CALLUM. it's hailing outside.

MIA. Well we could go into the house.

My dad's having his dinner but we could hang out in my room.

Not in a weird way.

It's just I dunno… There's a weird smell in here maybe?

Or atmosphere.

Do you think – would you mind if we left?

Cos it feels like, I'm really sorry if I'm being nosy or uh reading too much in to – yeah. But it feels like you guys might be about to uh… to have a misunderstanding or something.

You guys don't really seem like yourselves. You seem like different

And this is supposed to be somewhere that's safer than out there isn't it.

CATH. Mia stop it.

MIA. Cath, we can just go upstairs and I can make you a hot chocolate or

MIA grabs CATH's wrist and begins tugging her towards the door.

CATH. Get off me, Mia.

CALLUM. Cath I'm really sorry. I'll never do that again.

MIA. Please. We could have some – there's more coconut water in the fridge – I bought some extra cos I know you liked it.

CATH. Get off me. You little girl.

Pause.

MIA's heart breaks. She lets go of CATH's wrist.

Pause.

CALLUM puts his bat down.

CATH spreads her hands out as far as she can on the table.

MIA spots the the hundred-and-twenty-seven-year-old bottle of whisky. She picks it up. Holds it in her hands.

Then she gets it open.

Holds it up and begins to down it.

Some of it pours down over her tennis whites.

CATH and CALLUM watch.

Scene Two

CATH *and* MIA. *Their clothes are ripped, tied round their heads, etc. It's VERY hot.*

Rain and hail hammering the roof of the shelter.

The light is very low. Maybe it goes in and out.

Two silhouettes.

The clutter is almost all gone.

Maybe they sweep the floor.

Maybe they wipe down the table tennis table.

There's a rhythm to what they're doing.

Maybe CATH *starts drumming her fingers on the table and slowly this turns into some communal drumming?*

Just something ancient and ritualistic about their tidying.

This should go on for a while.

Eventually.

MIA. How long?

CATH. A minute.

MIA. Okay. I'm gonna…

CATH. Thank you.

    MIA *turns away.*

    (*Under her breath.*) Can you stay?

MIA. Pardon?

CATH. Can you stay?

    Pause.

MIA. No.

CATH. Okay. I'm sorry I asked. Thanks for… helping me clean.

MIA. Yeah.

CATH. Well I'll uh… afterwards we / could

MIA. Yeah. I uh… I've gotta prep my dad's breakfast so…

CATH. Okay well I'll pop my head / round the –

MIA. Yeah. Do.

Beat.

CATH. Thirty seconds.

MIA. Okay.

CATH. I'm so sorry, Mia.

MIA. That's okay. It happens I guess doesn't it.

CATH. What does?

MIA. People… I dunno.

Pause.

It's okay.

Pause.

CATH. Ten.

CATH *turns away from* MIA.

Nine.

MIA. Bye.

CATH. Bye.

Seven.

MIA *turns away from* CATH. *But she doesn't leave.*

The two women standing on opposite sides of the table with their backs to each other.

Six

Five

Four

Three

Two

One.

Silence.

MIA *looks over her shoulder at* CATH.

Nothing.

MIA *turns round fully.*

Eventually, CATH *turns round. She smiles sadly at* MIA.

Pause.

Suddenly CATH*'s body begins to do something incredible and terrifying.*

MIA. Cath?

MIA *starts moving towards her.*

CATH *snaps out of it.*

She smiles at MIA, *sadly. She was joking.*

It's better for a second then it's worse.

CATH. Well. Okay then!

Let's um…

What's left to clear?

Where's the… where's the Maybe box?

CATH *leans on the table.*

MIA. i don't know what to say.

Pause.

CATH. When does it happen?

Beat.

MIA. When does what happen?

CATH. never mind.

MIA. No. Tell me. I can understand. I know I can. If you just tell me.

Pause.

MIA *picks up a table tennis bat and serves the ball in.*

It falls on the other side.

Pause.

MIA *picks up another ball and serves it in.*

It falls on the other side.

MIA *waits.*

CATH *picks up a bat.*

come on.

we'll just do this

MIA *serves another ball in.*

CATH *returns it and they begin to rally in silence.*

The storm outside rages, pelting the tin roof of the bomb shelter.

Every now and then MIA *whispers her support across the table.*

it's just me and you

just serve it in – and yeah

there you go

The door blows open. Sound and light pour into the space.

The sounds of all the world. Traffic and tickets being printed and mugs being put on shelves and dogs barking at each other across the street and leadership contests and ships being waved off and wars beginning and phones ringing and YouTube stars introducing themselves and people kissing and children wailing and mothers finding their keys just where they left them.

They keep rallying.

Desperately.

We're just here.

We're just here.

And it's now.

We're just here

And it's now.

The doors blow closed again.

Yeah?

CATH. yeah…

MIA. Yeah?

CATH. Yeah.

Eventually, as they rally, the record player starts to turn.

Maybe the space begins to glow with light.

The song fades up slowly. The live version of 'Thunder Road'.

An announcer shouts: 'Ladies and gentleman, Bruce Springsteen and the E Street Band.'

CATH *and* MIA *stop and look at it for a moment.*

The harmonica kicks in.

Then they start playing again.

The ball starts looping higher and higher over the net, slowing the game way down.

Maybe the song slows down as well. Maybe it gets louder.

They play. It's kind of glorious.

Eventually:

MIA. What if she's me?

CATH. What?

MIA. Your mum. What if she's me?

What if I say it, and then it is?

Pause.

MIA *slowly goes over to* CATH *and puts the palm of her hand over her face.*

Pause.

CATH *puts her own hands over* MIA*'s, holding it there.*

They breathe together.

Silence.

AFTER

*When the lights come up it should feel almost blindingly bright
for a moment and then settle lower.*

We're in a park in St Petersburg on New Year's Eve 2020.

It's freezing.

There is the buzz of a crowd around MIA.

*Or perhaps instead of the buzz and flick of a normal scene
change, the house lights just click on,* MIA *turns to the audience
and immediately starts speaking to them. While* CATH *and*
CALLUM *pack up the table tennis behind her. All artifice gone.*

MIA. Hi Dad.

It's Me.

a.

Sorry.

Old joke.

I'm mainly just calling to wish you Happy New Year.

But I wanted to check to see whether you've rescheduled
your appointment at the neurologist's. I asked Raymond if he
could forward on the confirmation email but I haven't got
anything. He might still have my Hotmail address and not
my Gmail one.

I'll try to speak to him tomorrow.

Um.

I'm in St Petersburg for the Women's Trophy. I put it on your
calendar but you might not have switched over the month yet.

It doesn't begin for another couple of weeks but Dean
thought it'd be a good idea to come here and get some
competitive fixtures in while most of the attention is still on
the Australian tournis.

That girl Gina is here too and I'm staying in the same hotel as these two French girls who seem quite nice.

Did you know that in French the word for weather is the same as the word for time?

I think that must be really confusing on like a day-to-day basis.

But it's also quite nice.

Gina asked if I wanted to go in for doubles at some point.

I said I'd think about it.
And I am thinking about it.

Has there been any post by the way? When Grace moved down she said we would write long letters to each other like we were rich ladies from the fifties.

Grace.

Grace.

I've been *really* trying to enjoy my tennis again, so I was thinking about the first time you took me to play. We played for a bit then we went to that caff in Bushlake with the deer heads on the walls. It was a good day. Then it ended.

But I don't think you can put all the hope you have into one thing. Or person. Cos if you do, you might never come out again.

The fireworks begin to go off. But maybe there's no production indication of this. It's in our heads.

MIA *looks up at them in awe.*

Wow.

Sorry there are…

I know you can't see them but

The fireworks have started.

She watches them.

Silence.

But it was still a good day, Dad. Like… yeah. Even if I don't…

It was still a day that was good.

I dunno.

Maybe it's…

Maybe I'm not something that's finished.

Blackout.

Maybe we hear the sound of a sparrow flying out, through the doors of the theatre.

The End.

A Nick Hern Book

A Table Tennis Play first published in Great Britain in 2019 as a paperback original by Nick Hern Books Limited, The Glasshouse, 49a Goldhawk Road, London W12 8QP, in association with Walrus and Theatre Royal Plymouth

A Table Tennis Play copyright © 2019 Sam Steiner

Sam Steiner has asserted his moral right to be identified as the author of this work

Cover design © Ellice Stevens

Designed and typeset by Nick Hern Books, London
Printed in the UK by Mimeo Ltd, Huntingdon, Cambridgeshire PE29 6XX

A CIP catalogue record for this book is available from the British Library

ISBN 978 1 84842 900 0

Woodland
CARBON
www.woodlandcarbon.co.uk
NICK HERN BOOKS
Printed on Carbon Captured paper